CONTENTS

GENERAL LEARNING OBJECTIVES OF THIS UNIT

This Open Learning Unit will supply you with all the core information you need to answer an examination question or to write an essay on early socialization. It will take you three to four hours to work through, though if you attempt all the suggested activities, it may well take longer.

By the end of this Unit you should:

▷ understand what is meant by socialization and know about the main aspects of this topic;

▷ be familiar with the capabilities which all infants bring into the world with them and which serve as a foundation of social behaviour;

▷ know about the way in which the very first social interactions are managed by infants and their caregivers;

▷ be acquainted with the nature and development of attachments in the early years of life;

▷ and appreciate the role which early experience plays in the formation of an individual's personality.

1

The nature of socialization

KEY AIMS: By *the end of this section you will:*
▷ *understand what is meant by the concept of socialization*
▷ *know about the aspects of this concept that have been investigated*
▷ *have been introduced to the four major theories of socialization.*

What do we mean by socialization?

Children's behaviour, in the early years in particular, changes rapidly and at times dramatically. The aim of developmental psychology is both to describe and to explain such change.

We all take it for granted that children do change – after all, that is what childhood is about. If you meet a three-year-old whom you have not seen for the last year or so you will surely be struck by the extent to which that child has changed – in physical appearance, of course, but also in behaviour. You could then ask yourself just what specific changes have occurred during that year, and in this way *describe* the difference between one age and another. But in addition you probably also wonder just what accounts for these changes – in other words you want to *explain* the difference. It is here that the concept of **socialization** comes in.

Change is brought about by two sorts of factor: internal ones and external ones.

(1) *Internal factors* are those inherent in children themselves. They stem from the genetically-determined plan of development with which each of us comes into the world. When a baby becomes able to sit up at about seven months or begins to walk at around one year these changes are not brought about by other people's efforts; parents may encourage a baby to sit up and walk but they cannot teach it to do so. Instead, developments such as these, which take place in the same order for all human beings, are the result of **maturation**. This then, is the term used for the sequential unfolding of behaviour brought about by the internal programme which is part of each individual's inheritance.

(2) *External forces* shaping development originate in the child's environment, especially that part composed of other people such as parents. Teaching, training, setting an example, praising, punishing, encouraging – these are some of the ways in which other people impinge on children and, consciously or unconsciously, attempt to modify, channel, inhibit, promote and change their behaviour according to what they regard as desirable. This is *socialization*; its function is to convey to the child the appropriate **social norms**, that is, the rules or standards of behaviour that are approved by the particular society the child is reared in.

Let us therefore formally define socialization as ***the process by which a society's expected behaviour patterns, standards and beliefs are transmitted from one individual to another.***

But note two further points. First, maturation and socialization generally act *in tandem*. Take the example of learning to speak: maturation determines *when* children become capable of language acquisition; the particular language which they then begin to speak (English, Chinese, French, etc.) depends on the people around them, that is, on socialization. The one puts the child in a state of readiness; the other provides the content.

Secondly, socialization should not be thought of as something that adults simply impose on children. Such a *unidirectional* view held sway at one time in developmental psychology. Bringing up children was seen as analogous to clay moulding, that is, the newborn infant was regarded as a formless blob of clay which adults proceed to mould in any way they choose, until eventually the blob takes shape and sets – and hey presto! there is your finished personality. Such a view is wrong. For one thing, even the tiniest baby is far from passive and is already able to affect other people: think of the way in which a baby can immediately summon the mother to its side with a few blood-curdling shrieks. And for another, babies are not all alike but from the beginning have an individuality of their own to which their caregivers have to adapt. Talk to any mother with more than one child and she will tell you that what worked with the first one did not necessarily work with the next. So children's treatment does not just depend on the adult; it also depends on the child. A *bidirectional* view of the parent–child relationship is therefore more appropriate.

FIGURE 1. *Models of parent–child (P–C) interaction*

(a) What is maturation?
(b) What is socialization?
(c) Why is a bidirectional view of the parent–child relationship more credible than a unidirectional one?

SOMETHING TO TRY

As a quick check on the active nature of infants, observe the behaviour of a baby (about six or 12 months old) for a short time while playing with him or her. Make a note of all behaviour directed towards you. How many instances can be classified as a spontaneous 'initiative' on the baby's part rather than as a 'reply' to what you were doing?

Some questions to ask about socialization

There are five different aspects of the socialization process that we can usefully distinguish. They are concerned respectively with the questions what, who, when, why and how.

What is socialized? This aspect refers to the content of socialization: what are the behaviour patterns that are changed as a result of interacting with others? The range is vast, stretching from the relatively trivial such as parents' insistence on 'please' and 'thank you' (though what a battleground that can sometimes be!) to basic aspects of morality of the 'thou shalt not kill' kind. In each case we usually adopt whatever our society regards as the norm: the one-year-old may think it madness to use a spoon for eating porridge when using one's fingers is so much easier, but if others insist, well – so be it!

But as anthropologists like Ruth Benedict (1934) have shown, what is acceptable varies from one society to another. Take the Dobus of Melanesia: boys there are socialized to become ruthlessly competitive, so much so that adults positively encourage them to cheat and to lie in the pursuit of some goal. Just the opposite is found among the Zuni Indians of New Mexico. Here children are brought up to avoid all competition and conflict and develop co-operation instead. Someone who habitually wins races, for example, is barred from running because he or she spoils the game! Some social norms are universal; many others, however, are not, and even in our own society drastic changes in social norms occur from time to time and therefore in what we pass on to the next generation.

Who are the socializers? Think about the people who were mainly responsible for your socialization. For most of you the answer is easy: 'my parents'. Socialization may be about the transmission of society's norms, but society is an abstraction. Particular agents therefore fulfil this task and these are primarily a child's parents.

Yet even the reference to *parents* indicates a change over time, for only a few decades ago the answer to the question would probably have been 'my mother'. Previously fathers were somewhat distant figures, taking little part in the upbringing of their children. A scene such as that shown in Figure 2 would have been regarded as unusual. Now there is greater equality between the sexes: on the one hand more mothers go out to work, and on the other hand some fathers are much more involved in the day-to-day business of child rearing than they used to be.

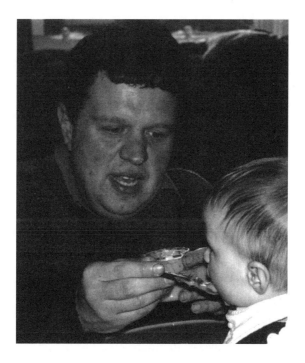

FIGURE 2. *Today's father*

But the list of socializing agents is by no means confined to parents. Their impact may be crucial in the early years; subsequently, however, children come under the influence of many other individuals: older siblings, relatives, teachers, peers and increasingly also the media, especially television. Each of these can influence the child in some way and so help to shape the developing personality.

Why is the family said to be the most effective setting for early socialization? Do you think young children brought up without a 'proper' family are likely to be at a disadvantage?

When does socialization take place? The answer to this question, you may well think, is obvious: in childhood, and especially so in the early years, with the possible exception of early infancy.

There is no doubt that it is in the period starting with the second year that parents are at their busiest encouraging, inhibiting, teaching and training. But in fact socialization begins as soon as the child is born and continues right through childhood, adolescence, and adulthood too. Even in the early weeks of life parents already make demands on the baby to adjust its sleeping and feeding patterns to what the adults regard as acceptable. And as far as socialization later on is concerned, consider the pressure that a teenager is under to conform when joining a new school or club or gang – conform, that is, to what that particular group regards as acceptable in the way of clothes, behaviour or manner of speaking. It is just the same in adulthood and is again most evident when joining a new group – a sports club, political party or regiment or even a new country to which the individual has emigrated. Each has its own traditions and expects all members to conform to these. Socialization, in other words, is a *lifelong* process.

Why do we socialize children? Here we are asking about the functions or *purpose* of this process. At its most basic, we need to ensure that society operates efficiently through everybody conforming to the same social norms. It is of little importance, for instance, whether we drive on the right side or the left side of the road, but is of great importance that all citizens of a country agree which one of these it should be. For that matter, manners – all those 'pleases' and 'thank yous' – are also important in smoothing the course of social interaction; they make people predictable to one another. Parents teaching manners to young children therefore teach them to live as members of a group.

As Carol Dweck (1986) has shown, there is even a socialization of occupational choice: boys are expected to go into 'tough' jobs like engineering or surgery, girls go into 'caring' ones like nursing or teaching. Such pressures to conform to particular stereotypes are undoubtedly at work, even though they often do not achieve their ends. (For further discussion of this, see the companion Unit on *Sex, Gender and Identity* by Patricia Turner).

How does socialization occur? We now come to the most difficult part, concerned with the processes whereby socialization produces socialized children. Let me warn you straight away that least is known about this aspect and that we therefore still do not understand how one of the most common and most important features of social life actually works. Not that there is any shortage of attempts to provide explanations. Below I have outlined the four main theories of how socialization occurs. Each is a highly intricate endeavour; here I merely want to draw your attention to their main features and the differences between them.

Psychoanalytic theory is surely the best known. But it is not just about dreams and sex and madness. Freud also tried to explain how young children come to be socialized by their parents. Children, he maintained, come into the world with all sorts of unacceptable selfish, destructive impulses. Initially parents control and check these, but in due course an internal self-control mechanism develops. This is the **superego** (roughly equivalent to our conscience), which contains the parental and societal values and attitudes incorporated by the child. Children are thought to incorporate these values by identifying with the same-sex parent in order to resolve deep unconcious conflict. The little boy, for instance, adopts the moral values of society as manifested in his father. Thereafter the child desists from 'wrong' behaviour because of the guilt that the superego generates.

Learning theory developed in part as a reaction to psychoanalysis, which was regarded as dealing with too many mysterious processes that could not be verified. Learning theorists therefore stress that psychology should be based on overt, observable events, and accordingly they propose that development is basically a matter of shaping behaviour by learning. The main way in which this occurs is through **operant conditioning**, that is, by reinforcing particular kinds of behaviour by rewarding them and extinguishing others by punishment. You must all have seen how a parent will praise a young child for being obedient but will get very cross if the child refuses to do as it is told. Obedience thus becomes 'stamped in' by the parent's actions.

Socialization, in this view, is therefore brought about by parents and others handing out rewards and punishments according to what they regard as desirable or not. Children soon come to learn the contingencies between their behaviour and the consequences that follow and thus come to learn the 'right' kind of behaviour.

Social learning theory, as formulated by Albert Bandura, is an extension of traditional learning theory and places particular emphasis on the process of **observational learning**. Children, that is, can learn the consequences of particular actions by simply observing others. Thus parents and others act as models and, depending on the effects produced by the action performed, children will or will not copy their behaviour. Of course not everybody observed will act as models; some individuals are more likely to be imitated (for example parents because of the child's emotional bond with them; pop stars because – well, because all young people seem to imitate them). Nor do children automatically copy what they observe; they may refine the actions according to their own evaluations and according to how they fit into each child's self concept.

Cognitive-developmental theory is based on the premise that social development proceeds as a consequence of sequential changes in cognitive (intellectual) development. A scheme for such changes was mapped out by the Swiss psychologist, Piaget, who proposed that children's understanding of the world differs according to the particular cognitive stage which the child has reached. The effects of parental action depend therefore on how the child interprets it, and that will vary according to stage of development.

For example, at three months, during the sensorimotor stage, the parent is just a bundle of sights, sounds and smells. At three years, during the preoperational period when children do not find it easy to consider any point of view other than their own, parents are there to fall in with the child's wishes. And not till later childhood, when a more mature appreciation of the world emerges, will children see parents as people in their own right with whom they can establish reciprocal relationships. The theory thus concentrates primarily on children's understanding of and thinking about their social world, and tries to explain how children intellectually interpret their parents' socialization efforts. (For further discussion of this, see the companion Unit, *Cognitive and Language Development* by Peter Lloyd.)

TABLE 1. Four socialization theories

Theory	Processes emphasized	Parental action required	Effect on children
Psychoanalysis (Freud)	Conflict resolution; identification with same-sex parent	Disciplining; checking	Development of 'superego'; internalizing standards; guilt
Learning theory (Watson; Hull; Skinner)	Conditioning; reinforcement	Rewarding and punishing	Learning specific behaviour patterns
Social learning theory (Bandura)	Observational learning	Acting as role models	Imitation
Cognitive – developmental theory (Piaget; Kohlberg)	Information assimilation	Explaining parental goals	Insight and understanding

In *conclusion*, the four theories (the main features of which are summarized in Table l) illustrate the attempts that have been made to answer the 'how' question about socialization. No one of them has been found entirely satisfactory: psychoanalytic theory has been accused of being too mysterious; learning theory is too mechanical and does not credit us with a mind; social learning theory is all right as far as it goes but, being confined to imitation, does not go very far; and the same goes for cognitive-developmental theory which also confines itself to just one set of phenomena, namely social understanding. Each has generated some useful research – and that, after all, is one of the important functions of a theory. But for a complete and satisfactory account we are still waiting.

SAQ
2

Summarize the main differences between the four socialization theories.

Social preadaptation

KEY AIMS: By *the end of this section you will:*
▷ *understand the meaning of social preadaptation*
▷ *have learned that infants from birth are perceptually biased to attend to the human face and voice*
▷ *know about the functioning of social signalling devices such as crying and smiling.*

There is ample evidence to indicate that from birth babies are, in a number of respects, already predisposed to respond to, and interact with, other people. Such inborn preadaptation shows itself in two ways:

- First, in various inherent *perceptual biases* that predispose infants selectively to attend to other human beings;

- Secondly, in a number of *signalling devices* designed to ensure the proximity of others and bring about social interaction.

Let us consider these two aspects in turn.

Perceptual biases

The attraction of faces

At one time newborn babies were thought of as perceptually incompetent, that is, as virtually blind and deaf for the first few days or weeks of life. With more sophisticated techniques, however, it has become possible to demonstrate that the range of perceptual abilities present from birth is in many respects very impressive. A young baby may not see the world the way that you and I see it and is not able to take in as much information, but, given the right conditions, the infant is far from insensitive to what goes on around him or her.

It has also become apparent that infants are by no means indiscriminate in what they look at. From birth on they attend on a selective basis, and by far the most fascinating object is the human face. This finding, as well as the technique for demonstrating it, comes largely from the work of Fantz (1961).By recording infants' visual behaviour under controlled conditions Fantz was able to ascertain not only *what* infants look at but what they *prefer* to look at. He achieved this with his **visual preference technique**, which involved placing infants inside a stimulus chamber, exposing them there to a pair of stimuli (for example, drawings, objects, patterns which the infant would examine) and then measuring the amount of visual fixation on each.

By this means it is possible to demonstrate that the human face (or representations of it) is easily the most attention-worthy stimulus object to an infant. As you can see from Figure 4, even very young infants are more interested in a disc with human features painted on it than in any other stimulus of similar size and shape, however brightly coloured or patterned.

FIGURE 3. *Fantz's visual preference chamber*

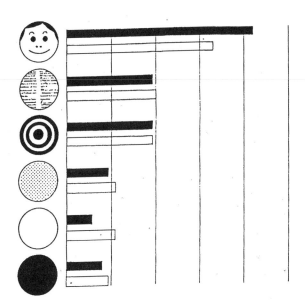

FIGURE 4. *Amount of looking by two- to three-month-olds (upper bar) and four-month-olds (lower bar)*

Does this mean that infants have some sort of inborn knowledge of the human face? Further research has shown that it is not in fact the face as such that has such a compelling influence but rather a number of primitive stimulus characteristics, inherent in the face but not exclusive to it, that account for visual preference. Look at Figure 5, illustrating the results of one of Fantz's studies. Three face-shaped stimuli were shown to infants: one (the 'real' face) containing the correct arrangement of features, another (the 'scrambled' face) also containing these features but in a scrambled form, and the third (the 'blocked' face) with a solid block of black at the top, of an area equivalent to that of all the features. As you can see, least attention was paid to the blocked face; however, the scrambled face turned out to be almost as attractive as the real face. In other words, it was not so much 'faceness' at this early age as the *patterning* of the stimulus that aroused interest, that is the fact that it was arranged in a number of separate features. Only later on do real faces assume a greater degree of attention-worthiness.

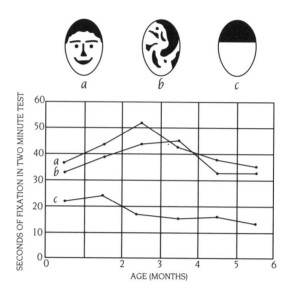

FIGURE 5. *Amount of attention to three face-like stimuli*
(from R. L. Fantz, 1961).

A POSSIBLE PROJECT

Repeat Fantz's experiment on the amount of attention paid to the three face-like stimuli in Figure 5 by babies in the first six months.
1. *Draw the three stimuli on pieces of stiff card.*
2. *Prop them up in front of the baby, two at a time, for half a minute.*
3. *Measure the amount of time spent looking at one of the stimuli; a helper should do the same for the other stimulus (if possible use cumulative stop-watches).*
4. *Repeat over a number of trials, randomly pairing the three stimuli.*
5. *Plot the average time spent looking at each stimulus.*

The infant's visual apparatus is thus attuned not so much to faces as such but to certain primitive stimulus characteristics that happen to be inherent in the face. As further research has shown, these also include:

— movement;

— three-dimensionality;

— symmetry.

Thus moving stimuli attract more attention than stationary ones; three-dimensional objects are preferred to two-dimensional ones; and symmetrical stimuli are looked at more than non-symmetrical ones. In short, faces are highly salient to infants because they possess a number of characteristics that are precisely those to which the infant's perceptual apparatus is inherently attuned. Together they ensure that infants are visually-oriented to their social partners from the beginning.

SAQ 3

Fantz's work on face perception shows that there is an inborn ability to recognize the human face.
— Correct?
— Incorrect?

Responsiveness to voices

Research on infants' auditory responsiveness shows an inherent sensitivity to particular stimuli. Again, it is human-like stimulation, that is, people's voices, that infants from the early weeks on find especially attention-worthy.

For example, John Hutt and his colleagues (1968) measured responsiveness to various types of auditory stimuli by recording the electrical activity of infants' muscles while listening. Speech-like sounds, it was found, elicited a far greater degree of responsiveness than other auditory stimuli, even though the infants were less than one week old. The structure of the human auditory apparatus at birth appears to be such as to ensure that the voice of another person is, from the beginning, a significant stimulus.

This differential responsiveness is basically due to the precocity of those parts of the brain which are specifically concerned with the production and comprehension of language. A newborn's **cortex** is, by and large, still very immature; some parts, however, are more advanced and these include the speech areas in the left hemisphere of the brain, shown in Figure 6. There are indeed intriguing suggestions that babies before birth are able to learn to make certain auditory distinctions. For example, in one study pregnant women were asked to sing 'Mary Had a Little Lamb' repeatedly during the last weeks of pregnancy. After birth, the newborn infants showed a clear preference for this song over another. Similarly it has been shown that newborns are able to distinguish the mother's voice from that of another adult female – again, presumably, as a result of prenatal learning. And one further sign of precocity: infants in the early months of life are already able to make certain distinctions within speech – distinctions that are meaningful to the processing of speech – long before the children themselves are ready to use language.

Thus from the first few weeks of life infants are able to:

— recognize speech sounds and differentiate them from non-speech;

— distinguish the mother's voice from that of a stranger's;

— distinguish some of the finer aspects of speech required later for the use of language.

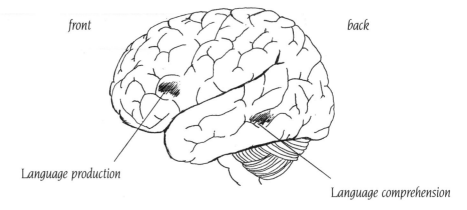

front

back

Language production

Language comprehension

FIGURE 6. *Language areas in the brain*

Social signalling devices

From the beginning, infants are equipped with certain means for attracting other people's attention. Among such **social signalling devices** two in particular deserve our attention: crying and smiling.

Crying

Have you ever listened closely to the crying of a baby? At first it all seems to be just a lot of noise and hardly a pleasant one at that, but gradually it will become apparent that there is a definite pattern to the cry and, moreover, that the pattern varies from one occasion to another according to the cause of the baby's distress.

What is apparent to the ear can be much more accurately investigated by means of **spectrographic** analysis – a way of visually displaying sound patterns. Thereby it has been possible to show that crying is a highly organised behaviour pattern which takes the form of a high-frequency **micro-rhythm**, that is, an apparently simple motor activity which is in fact organized in complex time sequences. Moreover, crying is really a generic name for a number of signals already differentiated from one another soon after birth. Three crying patterns can be distinguished:

- a hunger cry

- an anger cry

- a pain cry.

Each cry is made up of a series of temporal phases and spectrographic analysis enables one to measure these precisely. As you can see from Table 2, the three crying patterns show distinctive sets of temporal characteristics; in other words quite different information is carried by these patterns and most parents or caregivers can readily distinguish between them and react appropriately. Thus, by means of its cry the baby takes the initiative, indicates the nature of the particular problem and so is able to summon the parent to deal with that problem. So much for clay moulding! Not that such communication is intentional at first – for the first six or eight months crying is reactive; that is, the baby cries because (say) it has a pain. Only later on will it be able to cry *for the parent or caregiver* to deal with the pain. Reactive behaviour thus gives way to *intentional* behaviour.

TABLE 2. Characteristics of three cry patterns (time in seconds)

Cry phase	Hunger cry	Anger cry	Pain cry
Breathing out	0.62	0.69	3.83
Rest	0.08	0.20	3.99
Breathing in	0.04	0.05	0.18
Rest	0.20	0.11	0.16

SAQ
4

Explain in what respects infants' crying can be regarded as a highly sophisticated action.

Smiling

A baby's smile is invariably a delightful experience. When it first appears as a social response somewhere around the age of six weeks most parents are convinced it is special to them and that it shows that the baby now 'knows' them. In fact, as we shall see, it does nothing of the kind, though in order not to spoil their pleasure it would be as well not to tell any parents this.

FIGURE 7. *The charm of a baby's smile*

As various studies have shown, the baby's smile in the early months is elicited by stimulation which is much more primitive than the sight of another person's face. This has been established by taking the face to pieces, as it were, and presenting its various features one by one and in various combinations, either by covering up parts of a real face or by the use of drawings. In this way it can be shown that initially it requires nothing but a pair of eyelike dots to elicit the smile (as in Figure 8). Cover the lower part of a real face and the smile will appear as readily as when the mouth is visible. Cover the eyes, on the other hand, and the smile will no longer appear. If the face is shown in profile so that only one eye is visible the smile will also cease.

FIGURE 8.
Two eyelike dots to elicit smiling

The eyes thus represent the crucial eliciting stimulus, and initially these are indeed more effective than the whole face. It is as though young infants are innately programmed to attend to just one facial feature and become distracted by being presented with more information than they can cope with. In due course, however – partly as a result of maturation and partly due to increasing familiarity with people's faces – infants become capable of attending to more and more of the face, and (as shown in Figure 9) it then requires an increasing number of facial features to elicit smiling. At around seven or eight months the infant ceases to smile at faces as such and will now respond only to certain familiar individuals.

A POSSIBLE PROJECT
What makes babies smile? Test out the progression outlined in Figure 9 on babies between two and nine months.
— Draw two large dots on a piece of paper and hold it about 30 centimetres in front of the baby.
— Repeat adding more and more facial features.
— Note which stimuli elicit smiling in babies of different ages.

Inborn responses to particular stimuli, such as smiling or crying, are generally referred to as **fixed action patterns**, and the stimuli which release them are known as **key stimuli**. Ready-made stimulus–response links of this nature have considerable biological importance. In the case of smiling this importance lies in the fact that such an action brings the baby into contact with other human beings, that these others are delighted by the baby's smile and that the baby's chances of care, protection and survival are thereby increased. The smile thus provides another example of the child's preadaptation to social life.

SAQ
5

Complete:

The effective stimulus needed to elicit a smile from a two-month-old infant is ...
The effective stimulus needed to elicit a smile from an eight-month-old infant is ...

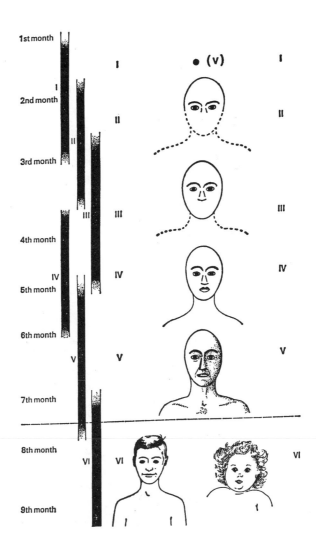

FIGURE 9. *Stimuli needed to elicit smiling at various ages*

3 Interaction and communication

> KEY AIMS: By the end of this section you will understand:
> ▷ how parents and infants manage to synchronize their behaviour
> ▷ what developmental changes occur in the nature of early social interaction
> ▷ what the respective roles are which adult and child play in such interactions.

Inborn characteristics such as those we have discussed in the last section enable infants immediately to participate in interactions with other people. The nature of such early interactions, the developmental changes that accompany them and the respective roles of child and adult have all been the subject of much research, designed to document in detail the child's entry into a social world.

Parent–infant synchrony

Any interaction between two individuals needs to be 'smooth', that is, the to-and-fro between them must be closely coordinated if they are to communicate efficiently or jointly achieve some task. How such synchronization is achieved at the beginning of life, in particular between parents and babies, can be seen from the following examples.

Hunger rhythms

One of the most obvious things about young babies is that periodically they become hungry and need to be fed. The feeding schedule is a matter of mutual adaptation: on the one hand the baby's hunger is based on certain internal periodicities; on the other hand parents have a timetable of their own (which includes, for example, eight hours uninterrupted sleep) that they would like the baby to fit in with as soon as possible.

Such fitting in can start very early on. This is illustrated by a study which investigated hourly changes in activity in two groups of infants during the first ten days of life. One group was fed according to a regular three-hour schedule, the other according to a regular four-hour schedule. After just a few days each group had already developed a peak of restlessness just before its respective feeding time – a finding which became particularly obvious when the three-hour group was subsequently shifted to a four-hour schedule and so had to wait an extra hour for the feed. The infants' hunger rhythms, it seems, had become socialized according to their particular experience.

Sleeping rhythms

Infants' sleep-wakefulness patterns also show the developing synchronization between parent and child. At the beginning, sleep tends to occur in many short periods, distributed throughout the day and interspersed by periods of wakefulness that are even shorter. Within a few weeks, however, both sleep and waking begin to assume a different pattern: individual periods become longer, they are less randomly distributed within each 24-hour interval, and in due course they become organized into a day–night pattern. As you can see from Figure 10, marked changes occur in the day–night distribution of sleep in the course of the first four months – brought about no doubt by parental pressure, however subtly applied. As with feeding rhythms, we can see an inborn pattern of behaviour change its temporal organization as a result of parents' actions – a very early example of socialization, designed, of course, to make the infant livable with.

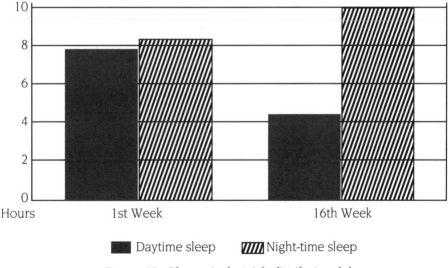

FIGURE 10. *Changes in day/night distribution of sleep*

Turn taking

Social adaptation takes place in many different ways. The two examples we have just discussed concern changes in behaviour relating to biological rhythms which occur over periods of hours. Other forms of adaptation occur at a much more minute, second-to-second level during social interactions, as seen in infants' sucking behaviour and in their babbling.

Sucking and maternal stimulation

As detailed examination has shown, the sucking response, especially during breast feeding, is another example of a highly complex inborn behaviour pattern. For one thing, it is closely coordinated with such other aspects of feeding as breathing and swallowing, and for another it is organized in temporal sequences which normally take the form of a *burst–pause* pattern: sucks, that is, tend to occur in series of bursts, with pauses interspersed between bursts (see Figure 11). Thus, like crying, sucking is a *high-frequency micro-rhythm* – a response that appears in particular sequences over very brief periods of time.

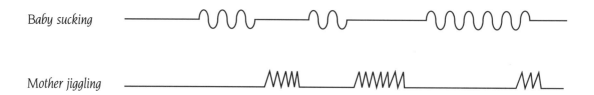

Baby sucking

Mother jiggling

FIGURE 11. *Baby's sucking bursts interspersed by mother's activity*

But sucking is only one part of what goes on during a feed. What the mother does is another part, and when her behaviour is investigated and related to what the child is doing it becomes apparent that one is witnessing a kind of dialogue, characterized by the two partners' *turn taking*. As Kenneth Kaye (1982) has shown, mothers tend to interact with their babies in precise synchrony with the burst–pause pattern of sucking. During bursts they are generally quiet and inactive; during pauses, on the other hand, they jiggle, stroke and talk to the baby, thereby setting in motion an alternating pattern in which first one and then the other is principal actor while the partner is spectator. The mother fits in with the baby's natural sucking rhythm, accepts the opportunity to intervene offered by pauses between bouts of sucking, and in this way takes responsibility for setting up the turn-taking pattern. Thereby she introduces the baby to a way of interacting typical of many that the child will engage in subsequently.

SAQ
6

Give examples of three inborn rhythms that regulate different aspects of infants' behaviour. What is similar about the three and what is different?

Vocal interchange

Just how skilled people are in interacting with others can be seen most clearly when we observe two individuals holding a conversation. Mutual adjustment here is essential: if both were to talk simultaneously communication would be virtually impossible. Turn-taking is required; speaker and listener need to exchange roles from time to time and do so smoothly and without overlap. This is generally done successfully, quite automatically, and with split-second timing.

Now listen to a mother and a baby (say of six or nine months) 'talking' together. The baby cannot, of course, use words as yet; nevertheless, one gets the strong impression that they are holding a conversation. The baby babbles; stops; the mother responds with some short comment; the baby resumes, and so on. In other words there is again a turn-taking pattern to be observed, and as shown by studies which have recorded such interactions, the exchange of speaker and listener roles is almost as precise as that among adults. Among adults, however, this is brought about by the *joint* action of the two participants; in the case of infants initially it is due very much to the mother's skill in inserting her contributions in the pauses between the infant's bursts of vocalizations. Thus, just as with sucking, the interaction starts with the infant's spontaneous behaviour; then the mother, by virtue of her sensitivity to the temporal patterning of her baby's actions, incorporates these actions into a mutual exchange, and in this way the impression of a 'proper' dialogue is created.

SOMETHING TO TRY

Observe the mother of a child under the age of one year 'talking' with her child. Listen carefully – do they take turns?

In fact, it would be more accurate to characterize early interactions as 'pseudo-dialogues', for the baby is not yet an equal partner who knows the rules of interaction (such as not talking while the other person is doing so). Instead, the baby sets the pace by means of its spontaneous bursts of behaviour and it is then up to the mother to reply, fit in and generally support whatever the baby is doing. Thus early social interactions depend on two conditions:

— first, *the temporal organization of an infant's behaviour* which allows other people to intersperse their contributions with the infant's;

— secondly, *the sensitivity of adults* to that temporal organization and their willingness to fit in accordingly, and in this way convert the encounter into a social interaction.

Adapting to a baby's behaviour (during feeds, vocal exchanges, etc.) is rarely a conscious, planned action but mothers seem to do this quite naturally and spontaneously. Does that mean there is such a thing as a 'mothering instinct'? And what implications would this have for fathers?

Topic sharing

In the early months social interactions are primarily face-to-face affairs: parent and baby looking at each other, smiling at each other, talking together. But around four or five months a marked change takes place: from then on the baby's encounters with other people increasingly occur around objects – third parties, as it were, that form the focus of the encounter. The change is largely due to the onset of manipulative abilities: being able to reach for and handle objects opens a new world for infants. The parent's face has become familiar and is no longer as fascinating; increasingly other objects form the topic of social interactions.

However, infants' attentional capacity is limited. Initially they can attend to only one thing at a time and not easily move from one focus to another. Thus they can play with the parent *or* with a ball; as yet they cannot play ball *with* the parent. It is therefore very much up to the adult to ensure that an *infant–object* situation is converted into an *infant – object – adult* situation; the adult, that is, needs to take the initiative in making the object a focus of *shared* attention.

There are a number of devices which we all use in everyday life in order to share with another person an interest in some object in the environment. Two in particular can be singled out:

- ☐ pointing
- ☐ gaze direction.

Pointing

Pointing is a particularly useful device for indicating to someone else what in the environment you happen to be interested in at that moment. It is a highly visible action and easy to follow. The ability both to *comprehend* other people's pointing and to *use* the gesture oneself is a social skill which first emerges towards the end of the first year.

FIGURE 12.

As to *comprehension*, it has been shown that infants less than nine months of age generally cannot follow the direction of a pointing finger. They look at the finger but then remain stuck there. After nine months or so they begin to follow the direction of the finger, but only under straightforward conditions, for example, when finger and target are close together in the visual field. Not till the beginning of the second year can infants locate most objects pointed out to them; it is only then that they become capable of appreciating the proper significance of this gesture.

As far as infants' *use* of pointing is concerned, this too does not emerge until the end of the first year. Let us note a number of features characterizing this development:

1. First, pointing *emerges at about the same age for all infants*, with no indication that it is in any way influenced by parents' example or teaching. Such spontaneous onset suggests the influence of maturation.

2. Secondly, it inevitably *takes the same form*. That is, the arm and one finger are extended. The finger is always the same one – the appropriately named index finger.

3. Thirdly, when it first appears the gesture is *not yet used for communication*: the infant points at the object but does not check whether the other person is following. Such 'pointing-for-self' is found at the beginning of the second year; 'pointing-for-others' does not appear until some months later. Only then is the social significance of this gesture properly appreciated by the child and used to influence others.

Thus pointing takes quite a long time to develop fully. Once it has done so, however, it is a most useful means of bringing child and adult together via a topic that they can share.

SOMETHING TO TRY

Do young children follow the direction of a pointing finger?
Try it out with babies from five or six months on. Place yourself right next to the child and point to a particular object. Note whether the child (i) takes no notice (ii) looks only at your hand (iii) looks in the direction of the pointing finger.
Also note whether the child points to the object.

Gaze direction

Ask a friend to stand on the pavement of a busy street and stare fixedly at the roof of a building opposite. Watch passers-by. I guarantee that a large proportion will turn their heads and look across in order to identify what is of such interest to your friend.

This example shows that gaze direction is another means of bringing about topic sharing. Just as with pointing, however, young infants cannot as yet appreciate the significance of such behaviour in another person; the ability to follow gaze direction does not appear until the end of the first year.

Until then it is the adult who follows the lead of the child. You can easily observe this any time you happen to sit opposite a parent with a baby on a bus, say, or in a doctor's waiting room: the baby's gaze has a powerful effect on the parent and acts like a signal to which he or she responds quite automatically by looking to where the baby is looking. They are now sharing a topic. However, this is often only a start in that it may lead to further interaction such as the parent pointing to the object, naming it, commenting on it and so elaborating on what the child chose in the first place.

Thus again we see that social interactions with young infants are frequently marked by the adult following the lead of the baby. Only after the first year, when another person's gaze direction becomes a meaningful signal to the child, will the onus for topic sharing no longer lie exclusively with the adult.

SAQ
7

(a) *What is meant by topic sharing?*
(b) *By what means is it brought about?*
(c) *What are the respective roles of adult and child in bringing about topic sharing (i) in the first year, (ii) thereafter?*

From nonverbal to verbal communication

As the child gets older the nature of communication changes, with a growing emphasis on the use of language. This is to be expected, for during most of the first year children can neither use nor understand language. Yet the extraordinary thing is that adults still talk to babies, even in the earliest weeks of life. Talking seems natural; can you imagine playing with a baby and all along keeping your mouth shut? In a study conducted in a maternity hospital by Rheingold and Adams (1980) the behaviour of nurses with newborn babies was observed. The outstanding feature noted was that everything they did was accompanied by talk. What is more, 23% of their utterances were questions that the babies obviously were not expected to answer, and 14% were in the form of commands, none of which the babies could possibly carry out.

It may be that being inundated by talk, day in, day out, will in due course help babies to acquire language when they are maturationally ready. In any case adults, when talking to a baby, tend to adopt a particular style that is quite different from that used when talking to another adult – a style generally referred to as **mother-ese** (or also as *child directed speech*) which is characterized by features such as:

FIGURE 13. *Mother pulling exaggerated face at baby*

- *Exaggeration*, as seen, for example, in facial expressions which are more emphasized than usual (for example, mock surprise) and in the pitch of the voice which is raised and has a wider range.

- *Slowing down* of rate of speech generally and of certain syllables in particular. Pauses between utterances are also longer, as though allowing for the limited information processing capacity of the baby.

- *Simplification*, as shown by the reduced complexity of speech: single words are used instead of sentences, and sentences tend to be shorter and grammatically simpler than in talk to adults.

- *Repetition*, both of speech phrases and gestures. The following excerpt of a mother's 'conversation' with her six-week-old baby illustrates this (as well as some of the other features):

'What's over there?'
'What?'
'Do you want to see something over there?'
'Oh you do like to look, don't you?'
'You really do!'
'You like to see what's out there.'
'What's over there?'
'Something over there?' (and so on for some time yet)

Such features make language more attention-worthy to infants and presumably easier to learn. But let us also note the following about 'motherese':

1. First, the term is really a misnomer: not only mothers but virtually any adult talking to a young child will adopt this style, hence the new term 'child directed speech'.
2. Secondly, *adults adjust their speech to the child's age*. As the child becomes linguistically more competent so speech becomes less simple, less repetitious etc.
3. And finally, the use of the style with children and its adjustment according to age are usually quite automatic and unconscious; they are just part of the 'natural' way of behaving with any young child.

Define 'motherese' (or 'child directed speech') and list some of its characteristics.

A POSSIBLE PROJECT

Do people vary their manner of talking according to the age of the child being addressed?
— Using a tape recorder, record a mother (or any other adult) talking to (i) a baby (ii) an older child, (iii) an adult.
— Listen to the recordings: how do they differ? Try to measure specific aspects (for example, sentence length) and compare the different speech samples. (This will be easier if you first prepare a written transcript).

4 Attachment

KEY AIMS: By the end of this section you will:
▷ have been introduced to the concept of attachment
▷ know about Bowlby's theory of attachment development
▷ have learned about work on plotting the developmental course of attachments
▷ have learned about the different types of attachment relationship.

What are attachments?

Have you ever seen a young child lose a parent in a crowded store or street? Or do you perhaps remember some early episode of being separated from your parents by, say, a sudden admission to hospital? If so, you will know something about the intense panic a young child experiences when losing the person whose presence spells security. The lost child may well be surrounded by kindly people trying to comfort him or her – but all to little avail, for they are strangers and the child only wants the particular individual to whom a bond of great emotional intensity has developed over the years.

It is this bond to which the term **attachment** has been given. An attachment may be defined as a *long-enduring emotional tie to a specific individual*, and is characterized by the following features:

- *Physical proximity seeking*, that is, an effort is made to maintain closeness to the object of attachment.

- *Comfort and security*, these being the result of maintaining closeness.

- *Separation upset*, that is, the severance of the tie produces distress.

- *Reciprocity on the part of the parent*, who in turn forms an attachment to the child (a process generally referred to as **bonding**).

Attachments can, of course, be formed at any age. However, it is the earliest relationships that have received most attention from psychologists. This is in part because of the assumption that the very first relationship formed by a child is a prototype for all subsequent relationships formed by that individual; but this remains an assumption and is not a proven fact.

Attachment

Bowlby's theory

The most comprehensive theoretical account of attachment formation is that by John Bowlby (1969). Attachment, according to Bowlby, is based on a number of inborn action patterns such as crying, sucking, smiling, babbling and clinging. These have emerged in the course of evolution because they increase the infant's chances of survival. Each initially functions like a *fixed action pattern* (a concept that we have already encountered in our discussion of the smile), that is, it is activated by certain quite specific stimulus conditions and then automatically runs its course until terminated. These inborn action patterns promote proximity to, and interaction with, the parent; the fact that they share this function entitles one to classify them together as **attachment responses**.

In the course of development several changes occur in this system. The following three are the most noteworthy:

1. First, a *progressive narrowing down* occurs in the range of stimuli that evoke attachment behaviour. We saw this in the case of smiling: initially anyone with a pair of eyes can trigger this response; eventually only certain specific faces will do. Similarly with other attachment responses: each becomes focused on just one or two specific individuals.

2. Secondly, once this occurs the various responses no longer function independently but become part of *one total behaviour system*. Crying, clinging, smiling and so forth are all used in the service of particular relationships with particular people. A distinction has therefore to be made between the separate *attachment responses* and the **attachment system**, which is an integrated network of responses, feelings and cognitions centered on the object of attachment.

3. Thirdly, the attachment system comes increasingly to function in a **goal-corrected** manner. A young infant does not vary its cry according to whether the caregiver is near or far, coming or going, attending or not. The older infant, on the other hand, is capable of continually adjusting its behaviour according to prevailing circumstances: it acts flexibly, intentionally and according to plans that will increasingly guide its behaviour towards some goal.

The attachment system is, of course, not the only behavioural system in the infant; there are also other systems such as exploration and fear, all of which are in continuous interplay with attachment. Consider a two-year-old going visiting with a parent. At first the child will remain close to the parent, perhaps clinging to him or her while inspecting the new environment and the unfamiliar people in it. But gradually the child will start exploring. The parent's presence provides security; a safe haven to whom the child can return whenever there is cause for alarm, such as a strange adult coming too close. Thus strangeness evokes attachment behaviour; being assured of the presence of the attachment figure, on the other hand, stimulates exploration.

In the first year or two the child's attachment is very much a matter of seeking the parent's *physical* presence. In time, however, children come to form what Bowlby referred to as **internal working models** of their attachment figures, that is, they develop an inner sense of the nature of these individuals, as well as of the relationship that the child has formed to them. As the child grows older, these internal models become more elaborated and will increasingly affect behaviour. Separation, for example, is tolerated much more easily when children are able to form an internal representation of the parents – they can relate to them in their absence without needing the continuous reassurance of their physical presence.

SAQ
9

Complete the following:
(a) An attachment *can be defined as* ...
(b) Goal-corrected *means* ...
(c) An internal working model *is* ...
(d) *The distinction between* attachment responses *and* the attachment system *is* ...

Developmental course of attachment formation

Bowlby outlined four phases in the development of child–parent attachments. The following table provides a summary of the characteristics of these phases.

TABLE 3. Phases of attachment development

	Phase	Age range	Principal features
I	Pre-attachment	0 – 2 months	Indiscriminate social responsiveness
II	Attachment-in-the-making	2 – 7 months	Recognition of familiar people
III	Clear-cut attachment	7 – 24 months	Separation protest; wariness of strangers; intentional communications
IV	Goal-corrected partnership	24 months on	Relationships more two-sided: children understand parents' needs

Let us pick out some significant aspects from this sequence.

Onset of specific attachments

How can one tell that a child has formed an attachment to a particular individual? One way is by seeing what happens when the child is separated from that person. If we go back to the example of the lost child mentioned at the beginning of this Part we get a very clear indication of the intensity of that child's need for the parent's presence. The child experiences considerable distress but other people will not do; only the parent's return will restore the child's sense of security. Thus *separation distress,* combined with evidence that people are *not interchangeable* as caregivers, highlights the existence of a definite attachment to a particular individual.

Using such indications it has become clear that the third quarter of the first year is the crucial period when children first show that their attachment behaviour has become focused on specific people. By observing infants' reactions to separation (for example, when left alone with an unfamiliar babysitter or when admitted to hospital) it has become apparent that up to the age of seven months or so infants show no orientation to the absent mother (or any other specific individual); as we can see from Figure 14, evidence of focused attachments appears only thereafter, as do signs of fear of strangers.

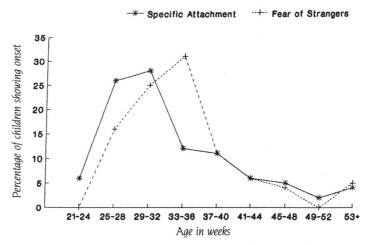

FIGURE 14. *Age at onset of attachment to specific individuals and of fear of strangers*

This is an important milestone of development as up to this point infants are, by and large, indiscriminate; caregivers are interchangeable and not missed when absent. It is only from about seven months that infants seek the proximity of just certain individuals and show wariness and proximity avoidance to others.

Prerequisites for specific attachments

What we see in the third quarter of the first year does not just happen out of the blue; it is based on other developments which make the onset of specific attachments possible. Two in particular are noteworthy:

— the ability to recognize familiar individuals

— the development of 'object permanence'.

(1) *Recognition*. We have already noted that infants learn very early on to recognize the mother and distinguish her from unfamiliar people – almost from birth with respect to the mother's voice; from about two months as far as her face is concerned. Such an achievement is clearly a prerequisite for the development of attachments to particular people; by itself, however, it is not an indication that an attachment has been formed. Being able to recognize the mother does not mean that the child will miss her when separated from her – other abilities are required for that.

(2) *Object Permanence*. Piaget, whose writings about children's cognitive development have been so influential, provided one particularly intriguing insight. According to him, infants in the early months of life are entirely dominated by the here-and-now; as yet they have no orientation to any absent object. In other words, they do not understand that something can have a permanent existence independent of their awareness of it – out of sight is literally out of mind. Infants do not yet possess the notion of **object permanence** – that does not emerge until the third quarter of the first year.

To demonstrate this Piaget used a simple hide-and-retrieve test (see Figure 15). A toy is put in front of an infant; just as the infant is about to take it, it is hidden by a cloth or a screen. Up to the age of seven or eight months the infant immediately stops searching for the toy and behaves as though it has ceased to exist. Only from that age on will infants remove the cover and retrieve the toy, so demonstrating that they remain aware of its continuing existence. Object permanence has been achieved. (For further discussion of this, see the Companion Unit, *Cognitive and Language Development*, by Peter Lloyd).

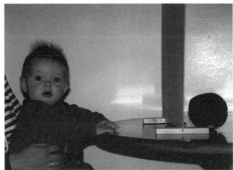

FIGURE 15. *Out of sight, out of mind*

SOMETHING TO TRY

Try out the hide-and-retrieve test with babies in the six to twelve months age range. Use any interesting-looking object and an uninteresting-looking cover (such as a handkerchief). Do the younger infants show the out-of-sight-out-of-mind phenomenon? How do the older ones respond?

You will appreciate that such behaviour is similar to the child's search for the missing parent and that it is dependent on the same psychological abilities. Separation is not a meaningful event to the younger infant because as yet there is no awareness of people in their absence. The older infant, on the other hand, recalls the parent's image when separated, remains oriented to the parent and shows this by crying for him or her. *Object permanence* and **person permanence** are aspects of the same development. Only when children can conceive of things as real, with an existence in their own right, can they develop lasting relationships to them.

SAQ
10

What is the relationship between object permanence and the development of attachments?

The objects of attachment

I have sometimes referred only to mothers as objects of infants' attachment. In the past, psychologists were in fact almost wholly preoccupied with the *mother*–child relationship – partly because it was believed that attachments grow out of the gratifications experienced during feeding (primarily a mother's responsibility) and partly because, at one time, child care was regarded as women's business, not men's.

However, it has been shown that attachments have little to do with physical gratification: infants form strong ties to individuals who have never fed them. And the rigid division between male and female family roles has been challenged: some fathers now participate far more in child care and infants thus have far greater opportunity to become attached to them. As a result, two things have become clear:

❏ For one thing, infants are able to form *several* attachments simultaneously and need not focus wholly on one person such as the mother. Fathers in particular are singled out, but older siblings, grandparents or other familiar individuals may also elicit strong attachments.

❏ And for another, the choice of attachment object does not depend on physical care or even on the amount of time spent with the child. Infants tend to be most attached to the people who play and interact with them and respond to them in a sensitive manner. The *quality* of social interaction, not its quantity, is the basis of attachment formation.

SOMETHING TO TRY

Ask some parents of young children:
(i) who the child is attached to (that is, with whom can it be left, or who can comfort it)
(ii) at what age the child began to dislike being left by the parent
(iii) at what age the child began to be wary of strangers.

Secure and insecure attachments

The assumption that the first relationship the child forms is a prototype for subsequent relationships has prompted examination of the nature of infants' attachments, with particular reference to the sense of security they obtain from the adult. In order to highlight variation of attachment security, Mary Ainsworth (1978) developed a procedure known as the **Strange Situation**. This consists of a series of brief, standardized episodes that take place in a laboratory observation room unfamiliar to the infant and that include being with the mother, being confronted by a strange adult, being left with the stranger by the mother, being left entirely alone and being reunited with the mother. According to Ainsworth, children's reactions to this situation can be classified into three basic types: *securely attached, insecure/avoidant, and insecure/resistant*. Table 4 gives further details.

TABLE 4. Types of attachment security

Type	Behaviour in Strange Situation
Securely attached	Child shows moderate level of proximity-seeking to mother. Upset by her departure, greets her positively on reunion.
Insecurely attached: avoidant	Child avoids contact with mother, especially at reunion after separation. Not greatly upset when left with a stranger.
Insecurely attached: resistant	Child greatly upset when separated from mother. On her return difficult to console; both seeks comfort and resists it.

29

These three types, it has been suggested, are considered by some to represent fundamental differences in the way social relationships are established. In particular, the degree of security in the first attachment relationship is thought to be the most influential ingredient in the creation of children's *internal working models* of relationships generally. For example, an insecure relationship with the mother, full of uncertainty and doubt about being loved, is regarded as setting the tone for all future relationships which that individual will also approach with doubt and lack of confidence.

SAQ
11

Explain the nature and purpose of the Strange Situation.

Why the differences?

Variations in the degree of attachment security could be brought about by different patterns of parenting. One has to be cautious here, for the evidence is by no means conclusive. However, according to Ainsworth, the principal cause lies in differences in *parental responsiveness*. Some studies have shown that the more responsive the mother is to the infant's needs in the early months, the more secure the child will be in the attachments found towards the end of the first year. How soon the mother responds to the infant's cries, how easily she recognizes signals in face-to-face play and how appropriately she reacts to cues provided by the infant during feeds – all these help to build up the child's trust in the mother. Maternal sensitivity therefore leads to child security. Mothers of insecure/avoidant infants, on the other hand, have been found to be 'psychologically unavailable' to their children, whereas those of insecure/resistant infants are likely to be inconsistent in their behaviour to the child.

What can be done to improve parenting so that we can eliminate, or at least minimize, behaviour problems such as insecurity in children?

Subsequent effects of attachment security

One reason why we must take seriously the security typology described in Table 4 is that it appears to be helpful in predicting a remarkably wide range of behaviour in subsequent childhood. These include:

• *Sociability*: Securely attached infants will subsequently get along better with peers, have more friends and be more confident with adults.

• Self-esteem: Securely attached infants are more likely to develop into children with higher self-esteem.

• *Behaviour problems*: Securely attached infants are less likely to show behavioural difficulties at later ages.

• *Task-related behaviour*: Securely attached infants tend subsequently to be more confident and independent in play and at work.

From all this you will gather that being securely attached as a baby is definitely a *good* thing! But let us not conclude that everything is determined by what happens in those early months of life. I shall have more to say about that in the final Part;

here let us note just two things. First, an individual's security classification is *not necessarily stable* throughout childhood: under certain circumstances (such as family disruption) it may change, though consistency over time is more typical. And in the second place, characteristics such as sociability, self-esteem, etc., are *multi-determined*: attachment security is only one factor among many that shape their development.

Deprivation and separation

> KEY AIMS: By *the end of this section you will:*
> ▷ *know the principal features of parental deprivation*
> ▷ *have learned about the effects of gross lack of individual care*
> ▷ *realize that intellectual and social development are affected by quite different aspects of deprivation*
> ▷ *understand why separation from parents can be so traumatic for young children*
> ▷ *be able to consider some of the practical implications of knowledge about deprivation and separation.*

What are parents for? You may think this a silly question, but in practice it has not proven easy to demonstrate just what effects the child-rearing practices of parents actually have on psychological development – largely because there are so many other influences, of which heredity is one of the most important. On the other hand, we do know that children brought up without parents may well be disadvantaged in their development, and such knowledge has been put to good use in improving the lot of many deprived children.

Parental deprivation

Previously referred to as '**maternal deprivation**' because of the exclusive (but unjustified) preoccupation with the mother–child relationship, **parental deprivation** basically refers to an *insufficiency of parental care*. The main points to note about it are:

— Lack of *psychological* care is the core component; this may or may not be accompanied by lack of physical care.

— Deprivation is seen at its clearest in *institutionalized* children, in particular those brought up in the large, impersonal orphanages common at one time.

— However, a child can also experience parental deprivation *at home*; that is, he or she may never leave the parents and yet be just as deprived of psychological care as an institutionalized child.

— A *wide range of effects*, including physical, intellectual and social effects, can follow deprivation.

Define parental deprivation.

We shall first look at some of the older studies involving more extreme degrees of deprivation and then go on to describe more recent work. In this Part our concern is with immediate effects; long-term consequences will be discussed in the next Part.

Effects of institutional upbringing

As a result of a number of classic investigations it has become clear that children reared under conditions of grossly deficient personal attention can become stunted in their psychological growth. Let us look at one of the best known investigations, that by René Spitz.

Spitz (1945) conducted his study in two settings, a foundling home and a penal institution for young women. Children in the former were mostly admitted soon after birth, having either been abandoned or orphaned, and were kept under conditions of grossly insufficient attention, as reflected in a staff–child ratio of only 1:8. The infants lacked toys, they were given no affection, their cries were not heeded and they were kept in their cots virtually all the time.

Infants in the penal institution, on the other hand, received a great deal of attention. Their mothers, who had been imprisoned for a variety of offences, had a lot of spare time on their hands and spent it mostly playing with the babies. Attention was thus both individualized and plentiful.

Spitz followed up both groups of infants throughout their first year and measured their progress by means of **developmental tests** – the baby equivalent, so to speak, of intelligence tests – yielding a **developmental quotient** (DQ) which is arbitrarily set at 100 to indicate average progress. As is clear from Figure 16, the infants in the foundling group, though starting at a relatively high level, progressively deteriorated throughout the first year, eventually developing severe learning disabilities. They also became depressed and unresponsive, and despite reasonable physical care were very susceptible to disease. The infants in the penal home, on the other hand, thrived in all respects despite also being institutionalized. Lack of psychological care thus appeared to be the crucial factor accounting for the deterioration of the foundlings.

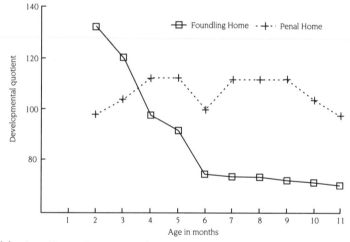

FIGURE 16. The effects of institutional rearing on Spitz's two groups of infants

Many people were initally sceptical of these results, partly because Spitz's study was in certain respects methodologically inadequate, but mainly because people did not *want* to believe that insufficient personal care could bring about such drastic consequences. However, other investigators obtained similar results, and there is now no doubting the reality of Spitz's findings.

Children in modern residential establishments

Nevertheless care must be taken that findings such as those by Spitz are not over-generalized. Not all children brought up without a family and living in an institutional environment suffer such consequences – it all depends on the institution! Indeed, because of these early findings, residential establishments for children have gradually become de-institutionalized and transformed into more stimulating environments. As far as *intellectual* effects are concerned, an upbringing in a Home (that is, an institution as opposed to a family home) need have no ill-effects.

This is well illustrated by a study carried out under the direction of Barbara Tizard (1974). It concerned three groups of four-year-old children who had spent most of their lives in residential nurseries. One group was still there; another had been adopted within the last year or so; while the third had been restored to their own mothers. The IQs (intelligence quotients) of all the children were obtained and are shown in Figure 17.

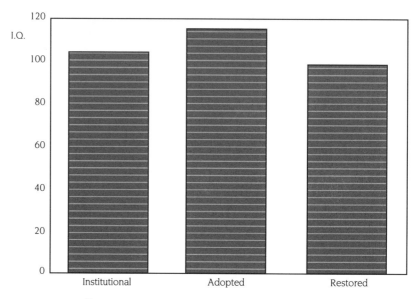

FIGURE 17. IQs of children remaining in the institution, adopted and restored to their own mothers

As you can see, there are two noteworthy points about these figures:

1. In the first place, none of the groups show any sign of learning disability (remember 100 is the average for the population). Despite the fact that they had spent so much of their early years in institutions, all were functioning normally.

2. And in the second place, the children remaining in the institution were performing no worse (even slightly better) than the children restored to their own mothers. When tested while still in the institution there had been no difference between the three groups. Subsequently the adopted children (most of whom had gone to 'superior' homes) had pulled ahead, but not so the children restored to their mothers. The reason for these differences lies in the amount of adult attention available in the three settings. Take one index of such attention, namely the percentage of children read to daily:

Institutionalized children: 69%

Adopted children: 67%

Children restored to their mothers: 25%

What can we conclude from these findings? First, that institutionalization does not necessarily mean intellectual deprivation. In the residential nurseries studied by Tizard the staff–child ratio was almost 1:1 – very different from Spitz's figure of 1:8. There was generous provision of books, toys and outings, and the general level of stimulation was thus vastly different from the institution described by Spitz. But we also see that being with mother is in itself no guarantee of superior functioning. The particular mothers who had their children restored to them all had considerable problems of one kind or another, and being under stress they were not able to devote much individual attention to their children – certainly not as much as the adoptive mothers.

It appears therefore that, as far as intellectual effects are concerned, it is the level of stimulation and amount of individual attention that matter. Severe deprivation, as found in old-fashioned institutions, produces severe learning disabilities. This does not mean, however, that all institutions are bad in this respect – on the contrary, some can actually be better than some homes.

(?) *In what ways would you set about improving a 'deprived' environment which was affecting children's intellectual development? Why would you choose these ways?*

Social consequences

It is largely due to John Bowlby (1951) that we have come to appreciate another potential danger of an institutional upbringing – one which affects social rather than intellectual development. Where that upbringing is *impersonal*, that is, where the child is not brought up by any consistent parent figure emotionally involved with the child, there will be no opportunity to form any stable attachment and the child's capacity for love may atrophy.

The **affectionless character** is the term used by Bowlby to refer to an individual who, as a result of parental deprivation, is unable to establish any permanent and meaningful bonds with another person – in love, marriage, parenthood or friendship. Having missed out on the opportunity to form stable attachments in the early years, the individual remains emotionally damaged.

There is some doubt about whether the link between deprivation and the development of an affectionless character is as firm as Bowlby suggested. For one thing, not all affectionless characters have had a history of deprivation, and for another not all deprived children develop such a character. But what Bowlby did achieve was to draw attention to the psychologically inconsistent and loveless upbringing to which deprived children are so often subjected. Barbara Tizard, as part of the study I mentioned before, found that the children investigated by her had, since admission to public care, been looked after by an average of 50 different people by the age of four-and-a-half. Imagine a four-year-old with 50 different mother-figures! There was clearly great inconsistency in these children's upbringing, and when people come and go in this fashion there is simply no opportunity to form any lasting bonds. Given such an upbringing it is not surprising that the children's emotional feelings about other people became blunted.

Thus one and the same environment can be good in some respects but bad in others. Institutions (such as Tizard's) can provide plenty of attention and stimulation and so help to foster *intellectual* development; the same institutions may provide such attention in a wholly impersonal manner and thereby impede *social* development.

SAQ 13

(a) What are the possible intellectual effects and the social effects of institutionalization?
(b) By what different aspects of deprivation are they brought about?

Separation

Whereas deprivation refers to *lack* of parental care, separation refers to its *loss*. We are thus concerned with children who have formed attachments but experience a break (temporary or permanent) in these bonds. This may occur when the child goes to hospital or is admitted to public care; it may also happen when it is the parent who, for one reason or another, leaves home.

Three response phases

The relationships which young children establish with their parents are generally considered so vital to their well-being that any severance of these bonds, even if only temporary, is regarded by many as potentially dangerous. However this may be, there can be no doubt that the immediate effects are often highly traumatic for children within the vulnerable age range. This range extends from:

– a lower limit of somewhere around seven months, that is, the age when children first establish attachments,

– to an upper limit of about four or five years, when tolerance for separation becomes greater as the need for the parent's physical availability lessens.

Various studies have provided detailed descriptions of children's behaviour when undergoing separation (mostly in hospital). They indicate the existence of three phases in the reaction to this experience:

Protest: The immediate reaction to sudden loss of a parent is distress, which can sometimes be very great indeed. The degree of desperation and panic can indeed be of an intensity that is difficult for an adult to comprehend. This phase can last for a few hours or go on for a week or more.

Despair: Overt protest gradually lessens; the child continues to cry for the parents but increasingly with signs of hopelessness. During this phase children become withdrawn and apathetic. Whereas previously they resisted attention from strange caregivers they now accept it passively and without struggle.

Detachment: Eventually children begin to cry less and to show some acceptance in their attitude to their caregivers.

These three phases form a fairly predictable sequence of reactions to the trauma of separation. Each represents a means of adapting to the intense stress experienced by the child. However, Bowlby (1973) believes that even the last phase, with its deceptive calmness, constitutes a highly undesirable pattern. According to him, the distress stemming from the loss of the parents has become so intense that eventually the child deals with it by repressing all feelings for the parents and, when finally reunited with them, behaves indifferently (that is, in a detached manner). If separation is prolonged and there are no opportunities to form attachments to others, the child is in danger of developing the 'affectionless character' that we discussed earlier.

SAQ 14

Relate the lower and upper age limits of children's vulnerability to separation to what you have learned about the development of attachments.

Daycare

Clearly separation experiences can be intensely upsetting to young children. Does this mean that children in the early years need the reassurance of the parent's constant availability? Is it necessary for a parent to be in attendance 24 hours a day?

There is now a large body of findings on the effects on young children of maternal employment and daycare. We can summarize these findings as follows:

• The great majority of studies have found *no differences* in any aspect of behaviour between the children of employed mothers and those of mothers at home.

• In particular, there are no indications that young children's attachment to the mother is any way diluted by not being with her all day.

• In certain respects children in daycare may even have an *advantage*, for example, in the development of independence.

• However, the outcome does depend on the *kind of substitute care arrangements* made, especially their quality and stability.

These findings underline the conclusion that it is the *quality* rather than the *quantity* of the mother's interaction with her child that matters. Obviously there has to be some minimum of togetherness. However, it is significant that many working mothers provide a more intense type of interaction in the time they do spend with the child than is normally found – a kind of compensating phenomenon.

A POSSIBLE PROJECT
Carry out a quick opinion survey based on the question 'How old should a child be before a mother goes out to work?'.
Compare the answers of (i) parents and non-parents (ii) employed and non-employed mothers (iii) the young and the not-so-young.

Some practical implications

Findings on deprivation and separation have had a considerable impact on the practice of child care. To illustrate, let us single out the following guide-lines, which arise directly from research, as they are being applied to children in care and to hospitalized children:

❑ *Children should not be removed from home except as a last resort.* Even in certain cases of child abuse, social workers try to keep the child at home while working with the parents. Paediatricians are encouraged to make use of out-patient treatment wherever possible.

❑ If the child is removed from home, *contact with the parents should normally be maintained*. To this end some children's hospitals provide overnight accommodation for parents and nearly all have liberal visiting hours. Similarly, social workers aim to keep children in touch with the parents with whom they are no longer living.

❑ *Substitute care for children should be as personal and stable as possible.* Thus children taken into care should preferably go to foster homes; residential homes, if used, should be small and intimate and each child should be assigned his or her own 'houseparent'.

(?) *There are lots of 'common sense' ideas about bringing up children, that is, beliefs people adopt quite spontaneously as 'correct'. When such ideas clash with the conclusions from research, should one back common sense or research?*

Long-term effects of early experience

> KEY AIMS: By *the end of this section you will:*
> ▷ understand what is meant by *critical periods of development*
> ▷ know *why one must doubt the usefulness of this concept*
> ▷ appreciate *that the effects of early experience need not be permanent but can be reversed under certain conditions.*

Are the early years the most important ones? Is it then that children are most impressionable and affected for life by whatever experiences they have?

This issue has been debated fiercely and for a long time. Freud certainly had no doubts: he believed firmly that the early years are formative, that unpleasant experiences ('infantile trauma') may permanently affect the individual, and that much of adult neurosis can thus be traced back to these early origins. But however influential Freud's theories may be they are, after all, nothing but unconfirmed assumptions. For one thing, Freud's data were derived solely from individual case studies of disturbed people in treatment rather than from scientifically-conducted, formal investigations. And for another, Freud himself never studied children but relied on the retrospective accounts of adults – not the most reliable method of obtaining information about what goes on in the early years. It therefore becomes important to see what other writers using different approaches had to say about this issue.

SOMETHING TO TRY

What is the popular view about the importance of the early years? Ask some parents, preferably of older or grown-up children, which years they consider to be the most important ones in the development of their children, and why.

The critical period hypothesis

One influential line of thought has come from investigations of the **critical period** hypothesis – the belief that there is a limited period of time in early life when individuals are maximally susceptible to certain kinds of experiences which leave permanent and irreversible effects on them. Originating in studies of animals, this hypothesis has also been applied to human development.

Animal studies

Konrad Lorenz, a zoologist credited with founding the discipline of ethology (that is the scientific study of animal behaviour) showed that among birds such as geese, ducks and chickens, the young, once they are hatched from the egg, follow the first moving object they encounter (normally the mother) and continue to remain near it. Lorenz referred to this phenomenon as **imprinting**, regarding it as a special form of learning which ensures that the young animal always remains in the proximity of its caretaker – its source of protection and food. But although the mother is the biologically 'correct' object, Lorenz demonstrated that imprinting can also occur with a wide range of quite inappropriate objects, for example, toy trains, footballs and even himself – whatever the animal first comes into contact with.

In addition, Lorenz also proposed that imprinting can only occur within a particular relatively short time period, typically lasting just a few hours in the case of the birds he studied (as shown for chicks in Figure 18). Whatever the animal learns to follow during this time represents a permanent and irreversible attachment. If, say, a gosling becomes imprinted on a human being, it cannot subsequently shift its affections to a goose; if it is kept in isolation and forms no attachments at this time, it will remain a social isolate all its life.

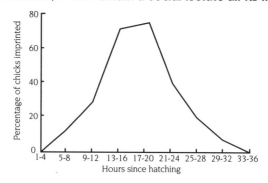

FIGURE 18. *The critical period for imprinting of chicks*

Later work has shown that things are not quite as clear cut as Lorenz had suggested and that critical periods are not as critical as was first believed. Animals may be more susceptible to certain kinds of experience at some periods of development than at others; on the other hand it has also been shown that, given the right conditions, the effects can subsequently be reversed. As a result, the term **sensitive periods** is now preferred. However, when they first appeared, Lorenz's ideas had considerable influence on thinking about not only animal but also human development.

What is the use of animal studies in dealing with issues such as the effects of early experience on human development?

Are there critical periods in human development?

As we have already seen, John Bowlby suggested that a child deprived of the opportunity to form attachments will develop an affectionless character, that is, be permanently unable to establish meaningful relationships with others. But, inspired by Lorenz's findings, Bowlby further proposed that the opportunity to form attachments *must* occur in a sharply delimited period early on. Citing as evidence a series of studies of children who had spent their first few years in institutions before being fostered, he declared that:

'*Even good mothering is almost useless if delayed until after the age of two-and-a-half years*' (Bowlby, 1951)

It follows that the formation of the first attachment can be delayed beyond the first year, but that there is nevertheless a definite limit beyond which no amount of the 'right' kind of experience is effective if the child has already been deprived; the child is bound to develop the affectionless character. According to Bowlby, the first two-and-a-half years constitute a critical period for attachment formation: whatever happens or does not happen then will affect the individual for ever after.

Describe the critical period hypothesis.

Reversible or irreversible?

Freud, Lorenz and Bowlby between them ensured that for a long time there was firm belief in the permanency of effects resulting from early experience. We are shaped for good or ill, so it was thought, by what happens to us right at the beginning of life. Thereafter, we are prisoners of our past.

More recently, however, this whole issue has had to be considered anew. Evidence from a number of empirical studies has shown that the effects of early experience are not necessarily permanent; that given the right conditions it is possible to reverse them. Let us look at two such studies, dealing with social and intellectual effects respectively.

Tizard's adoption study

Given Bowlby's assertion about the necessity to form the first social relationship early on, it becomes essential to investigate what happens to children who were deprived of the chance to develop attachments in early life but did have the opportunity subsequently. Can such children still form attachments?

The answer comes from the study by Barbara Tizard that we have already referred to. You will recall that she investigated children who had been institutionalized more or less from birth, who were cared for by so many different individuals that they had no chance of forming attachments to any of them, and some of whom subsequently left the institution and were adopted. These adoptions were all late ones, occurring around three to four years of age and in one or two cases not till seven years. All, that is, took place well after the age of two-and-a-half, the proposed upper limit of the critical period for attachment formation.

Tizard followed up these children and investigated their development and adjustment at age eight. The crucial findings for us concern the relationships with their adoptive parents and can be summarized as follows:

- Nearly all had formed close attachments to the parents.

- Even the oldest children at adoption had made a successful adjustment.

- None resembled the description of the affectionless character.

This picture was confirmed when the children were seen again at age 16. It appears, therefore, that failure to form attachments early on does *not* necessarily lead to a later inability to form relationships; the existence of a critical period confined to the first two or three years of life must thus be questioned; and the notion that early experience leads to irreversible consequences receives no support from these findings.

Wayne Dennis's Crèche study

One of the studies supporting Spitz's findings on the effects of severe deprivation, discussed in the previous Part, was carried out by Wayne Dennis (1973). The particular institution he worked in (referred to as the Crèche) was located in the Lebanon and was, if anything, even more depriving than Spitz's Foundling Home (see Figure 19). As a result, Dennis too observed progressive deterioration to occur throughout infancy – from an average DQ of 100 at the beginning of the first year to a mere 53 at the end of the first year (that is, twelve-month-old infants were functioning at the level of six-month-old infants). What is more, these severe disabilities continued; for example, more than half the children were still not able to sit up at 21 months of age (usually accomplished around seven months) and less than 15% were able to walk by the age of three.

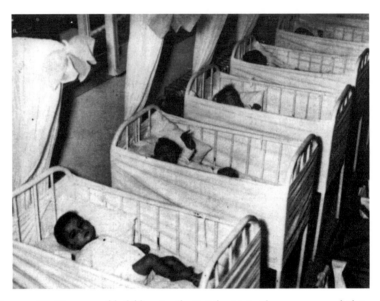

FIGURE 19. *Two-year-old children in the Crèche. Note the screens round their cots, depriving them of visual stimulation.*

A number of years later, when the children were in their teens, Dennis returned to the Lebanon and managed to trace his original group. At the age of six most of the children had been transferred from the Crèche to institutions more suitable for older children – the girls to one and the boys to another. The remainder had been adopted straight from the Crèche. All were given intelligence tests; the IQs obtained are given in Figure 20.

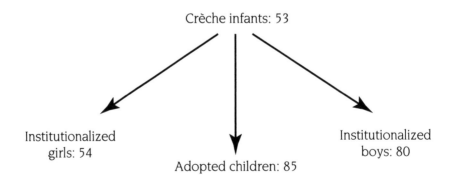

FIGURE 20. *IQs of children in Dennis's study*

As you see, there is a marked difference between the scores of the institutionalized boys and the girls. The girls had not improved since infancy and obviously had severe learning difficulties. The boys, on the other hand, though below average, nevertheless performed well within the normal range. This applies also to the adopted children – in fact those adopted before the age of two obtained an average IQ of 96 in their teens.

Why the difference between the institutionalized girls and the other two groups? The answer lies in the *kind of environment* to which they had been transferred after leaving the Crèche. The girls' institution was every bit as barren as the Crèche; their deprivation simply continued. The boys' institution was much more stimulating: it was better staffed, it had far more educational and recreational facilities and the children received much more individual attention. This applied, of course, even more so to the adopted children who lived normal family lives.

Thus, despite the extremely severe effects observed early on, those children who had later been placed in favourable environments were functioning normally. Although, for the most part, the change in their regime did not take place till they were six years old, there was no indication that the damage brought about by their early experience could not be reversed.

Some lessons to be learned

Let us summarize what the studies of Tizard and Dennis tell us:

• *Early experience need not leave permanent effects,* however early and however severe that experience may be.

• *Effects can only be reversed by a drastic change in life exerience.* Tizard's adopted children were cared for by permanent and loving parents for the first time; the boys and the adopted group in Dennis's study were transferred to environments considerably more stimulating than what they had been used to.

• We *do not know if age limits do exist beyond which one can no longer reverse the effects of earlier experience.* The oldest children in Tizard's group were seven when adopted; transfer of Dennis's children took place at six. We have, as yet, no information about the fate of children older at the point of transition. In the meantime, however, it is surely best to go on the assumption that *it is never too late!* That way at least one will never consider anyone as being too old for help.

SAQ 16

Does early experience leave permanent effects?

Some concluding thoughts

The early years are important – but so are all the later ones. Early experience lays the foundations for personality development but, as we have seen, it can be disconfirmed by subsequent experience. Thus one cannot maintain that children are necessarily more vulnerable at some ages than at others. Research on the impact of life experiences such as parental divorce or natural disasters (earthquakes, typhoons, etc.) shows that younger children differ from older ones in the *nature and not the degree* of psychological consequences.

The conclusion is therefore much more optimistic than would follow from the views of Freud, Lorenz and Bowlby: however horrific their early experience may have been, people are not inevitably trapped thereby. The eventual outcome depends not just on what happened early on but also on subsequent events; these may *reinforce* earlier events but they may also *reverse* their effects. All is not lost by any means if the early years are deficient in some way; even quite young children do have considerable rallying powers.

FURTHER READING

BOWLBY, J. (1969) *Attachment*. Harmondsworth: Penguin. (A classic and comprehensive statement of attachment theory.)

LEACH, P. (1983) *Babyhood*, 2nd ed. Harmondsworth: Penguin. (A general look at the first two years, written mainly for parents but based on research.)

RUTTER, M. (1981) *Maternal Deprivation Reassessed*, 2nd ed. Harmondsworth: Penguin. (Useful not only for its account of deprivation and separation but also for its statement about normal development.)

SCHAFFER, R. (1977) *Mothering*. Glasgow: Fontana. (A short overview of work on the nature and effects of mothering and child rearing.)

SCHAFFER, H.R. (1990) *Making Decisions About Children: Psychological Questions and Answers*. Oxford: Blackwell. (A book designed to aquaint practitioners with research about children's social development and family relationships.)

STERN, D. (1977) *The First Relationship*. Glasgow: Fontana. (A popular account of the establishment of mother–infant synchrony.)

REFERENCES

Students studying psychology at pre-degree level, whether in schools, FE colleges or evening institutes, seldom have access to a well-stocked academic library; nor is it expected that they will have consulted all the original references. For most purposes, the books recommended in Further Reading will be adequate. This list is included for the use of those planning a full-scale project on this topic, and also for the sake of completeness.

AINSWORTH, M.D.S. (1973) The development of infant – mother attachment. In B.M.C. Caldwell and H.N. Ricciuti (Eds) *Review of Child Development Research*, Vol. 3. Chicago: University of Chicago Press.

AINSWORTH, M.D.S., BLEHAR, M.C., WATERS, E. and WALL, S. (1978) *Patterns of Attachment*. Hillsdale, N.J: Lawrence Erlbaum.

BENEDICT, R. (1934) *Patterns of Culture*. Boston: Houghton Mifflin.

BOWLBY, J. (1951) *Maternal Care and Mental Health*. Geneva: World Health Organisation. (Also published as *Child Care and the Growth of Love* (1964) Harmondsworth: Penguin.)

BOWLBY, J. (1969) *Attachment and Loss*, Vol 1. *Attachment*. London: Hogarth Press. (Also published by Penguin.)

BOWLBY, J. (1973) *Attachment and loss*, Vol 2. *Separation: Anxiety and Anger*. London: Hogarth Press.

BREMNER, J.G. (1988) *Infancy*. Oxford: Blackwell.

CLARKE, A.M., CLARKE, A.D.B. (1976) *Early Experience: Myth and Evidence*. London: Open Books.

CLARKE-STEWART, A. (1982) *Daycare*. Glasgow: Fontana.

DENNIS, W. (1973) *Children of the Crèche*. New York: Appleton-Century- Crofts.

DUNN, J. (1984) *Sisters and Brothers*. Glasgow: Fontana.

DWECK, C. (1986) Motivational processes affecting learning. *American Psychologist*, 41, 1040–1048.

FANTZ, R.L. (1961) The origin of form perception. *Scientific American*, 204, 66–72.

FOGEL, A. (1991) *Infancy. 2nd ed*. St Paul, Minnesota: West.

GRUSEC, J.E. and LYTTON, H. (1988) *Social Development*. New York: Springer.

HUTT, S. J., HUTT, C., LENARD, H.G., BERNUTH, H. V., and MUNTJEWERFF, W. J. (1968) Auditory responsivity in the human neonate. *Nature*, 218, 888–890.

KAYE, K. (1982) *The Mental and Social Life of Babies*. London: Methuen.

LEWIN, R. (1975) *Child Alive*. London: Temple Smith.

MACCOBY, E.E. (1980) *Social Development*. New York: Harcourt Brace Jovanovich.

MAURER, D. and MAURER, C. (1990) *The World of the Newborn*. Harmondsworth: Penguin.

MURPHY, C.M. and MESSER, D.J. (1977) Mothers, infants and pointing: a study of a gesture. In Schaffer, H.R. (Ed) *Studies of Mother–Infant Interaction*. London: Academic Press.

PARKE, R.D. (1981) *Fathering*. Glasgow: Fontana.

PARKE, R.D. (Ed.) (1984) *The Family: Review of Child Development Research*. Chicago: University of Chicago Press.

RHEINGOLD, H.L. and ADAMS, J.L. (1980) The significance of speech to newborns. *Developmental Psychology*, 16, 397-403.

ROSENBLITH, J.F. (1992) *In the Beginning, 2nd ed*. London: Sage.

SCARR, S. and DUNN, J. (1987) *Mother Care/Other Care*. Harmondsworth: Penguin.

SCHAFFER, H.R. (1984) *The Child's Entry into a Social World*. London: Academic Press.

SLATER, A. and BREMNER, G. (Eds) (1989) *Infant Development*. Hove: Lawrence Erlbaum.

SLUCKIN, W. (1972) *Imprinting and Early Learning, 2nd ed*. London: Methuen.

SLUCKIN, W., HERBERT, M. and SLUCKIN, A. (1983) *Maternal Bonding*. Oxford: Blackwell.

SNOW, C.E. (1977) The development of conversation between mothers and babies. *Journal of Child Language*, 4, 1 – 22.

SPITZ, R.A. (1945) Hospitalism: an inquiry into the genesis of psychiatric conditions in early childhood. *Psychoanalytic Study of the Child*, I, 53 – 74.

TIZARD, B. (1977) *Adoption: A Second Chance*. London: Open Books.

TIZARD, B. and REES, J. (1974) A comparison of the effects of adoption, restoration to the natural mother and continued institutionalization on the cognitive development of four-year-old children. *Child Development*, 45, 92-99.

WACHS, T.D. and GRUEN, G.E. (1982) *Early Experience and Human Development*. New York: Plenum.

WOLFF, P.H. (1969) The natural history of crying and other vocalization in early infancy. In Foss, B.M. (Ed) *Determinants of Infant Behaviour*, Vol. 4. London: Methuen.

ANSWERS TO SELF-ASSESSMENT QUESTIONS

SAQ 1 (a) Maturation is development as a result of internal forces, based on the inherited programme with which we all come into the world.

(b) Socialization is development as a result of external forces, with particular reference to other people's efforts to get the individual to conform to the demands of society.

(c) For one thing, because even the youngest baby is far from passive but can influence adults' behaviour, for instance by crying. And for another, because the nature of that influence varies according to the child's individuality, for example some babies cry more than others and will affect adults accordingly.

SAQ 2 The main difference lies in the means of socialization which each theory focuses on. These are:

– For psychoanalytic theory: identification with the same-sex parent whose standards are internalized and form the superego.

– For learning theory: the shaping of behaviour through learning the consequences (reward or punishment) of particular actions.

– For social learning theory: the imitation of the actions performed by other people who serve as models.

– For cognitive-developmental theory: intellectual understanding of adults' socialization efforts necessary.

SAQ 3 Incorrect, because it is not the face as such but rather various, more primitive, aspects (patterning, movement, etc.) inherent in faces that are attention-worthy to the young infant.

SAQ 4 It is sophisticated because (a) it is organized in complex time sequences and (b) these sequences differ from one type of cry to another and so convey different information to listeners. But it is *not* sophisticated in the early months of life as it is purely reactive rather than intentional.

SAQ 5 ...a pair of eye-like dots.

...the face of a specific, familiar person.

SAQ 6 (i) Hunger rhythms; (ii) sleeping rhythms; (iii) sucking rhythms. They are similar in that all are inborn cycles of behaviour; they are different in the length of their periodicity: three or four hours for hunger; 24 hours for sleep; a few seconds for sucking.

SAQ 7 (a) Topic sharing is any form of social interaction around an object (as opposed to only face-to-face interaction).

(b) Through following another person's pointing or gazing (later on also by verbal reference, for example, 'Just look at x').

(c) (i) In the first year the child cannot yet understand the significance of pointing or gazing and it is therefore the adult who mostly follows the lead of the child.

(ii) Thereafter the child is increasingly able to follow such gestures and the roles of the two partners become more equal.

SAQ 8 Motherese (or child directed speech) is a special style adopted by adults (not only mothers) when talking to young children. It is characterized by features such as exaggeration, slowing down, simplification and repetition, all of which become less marked as the child becomes older and more competent linguistically.

SAQ 9 (a) ...a long-enduring, emotionally meaningful tie to a specific individual.

(b) ...acting intentionally, flexibly and according to some plan.

(c) ...a mental representation of the other person.

(d) Attachment responses are the overt actions which bring about proximity between infant and adult and which can at first be elicited by quite different people, whereas an attachment system is an integrated network containing all the responses, feelings and cognitions that are focused on some specific person.

SAQ 10 Object permanence (or person permanence) is a prerequisite to the development of attachments. The child cannot form lasting relationships to other persons until these persons are known to exist even when they are absent.

SAQ 11 The Strange Situation, devised by Mary Ainsworth, consists of a series of episodes in an unfamiliar room. They include being with the mother, being with a stranger, being left by the mother and then reunited with her. The purpose of this procedure is to highlight individual differences in the security of children's attachment relationships.

SAQ 12 Parental deprivation is insufficiency of parental care. It refers to psychological aspects of care and may or may not be accompanied by lack of physical care.

SAQ 13 (a) Intellectual effects are to be seen in the development of learning disabilities (as measured by DQs and IQs). Social effects are found in lack of attachment formation, whether permanent (that is, an inability to form attachments – the 'affectionless character') or temporary.

(b) Intellectual effects are brought about by lack of stimulation. Social effects are brought about by lack of consistant personal care from one particular individual.

SAQ 14 The lower limit is around six or seven months because it is not till then that children become cognitively able to form lasting relationships with others and can think of them even when out of sight. By four or five years children's mental representations of others are sufficiently advanced to enable them fully to relate to others over lengthy periods of absence without a feeling of having been abandoned.

SAQ 15 The critical period hypothesis proposes that there is a sharply defined time period, usually in early life, when the individual is maximally susceptible to certain kinds of experience which are likely to leave permanent effects.

SAQ 16 Only if it is subsequently reinforced (as happened with Dennis's girls). A change in life experience (as occurred in the case of Dennis's boys) can modify and reverse earlier effects.